From Paw Paw to Sesame: My Journey

Written by Dr. Loretta Moore Long and Scott Alboum
Book Designer Scott Alboum

When my daddy Verle graduated to heaven, my brother

Charles and my sister Cyndi found many of these photos

in his desk. The photos they found along with some I owned

helped to tell the story of how I Occupied My Dream.

That means to live your dream OUT LOUD.....Not Just In Your Head.

Thanks for reading my book!

REMEMBER: Keep On Trying 'Til You Find Out Where You FIT!.

Keep On Trying, JUST DON'T QUIT!!!

Love.....Dr. Loretta Moore Long

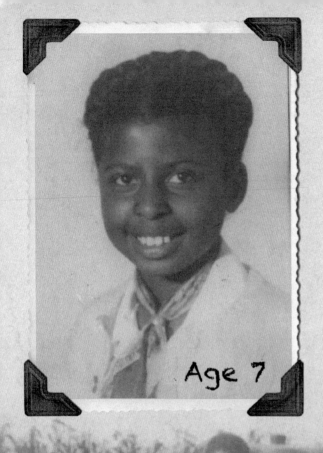

Age 7

Our family farm in the 1950s.

Our whole family worked on the farm everyday.

My Mom, Marjorie

That's me

Charlie, My Little Brother

September 15, 1953

They told me I wasn't good enough.

I know I sing good enough!

There's always choir.

Not getting picked will not stop me from occupying my dream!

Debate Team

CLASS BROWNIES

1956 Yearbook Staff

Newspaper Staff

This was the day I earned a music scholarship.

Paw Paw High School Varsity Choir

An original song by Loretta Moore

Keep On Trying 'Til You Find Out Where You FIT!
Keep On Trying, JUST DON'T QUIT!!!

I never let anyone discourage me. I always kept trying out for things. My high school music teacher, Mr. Hahnenberg, gave me my first paid singing job. I went from making fifty cents an hour as a babysitter to making fifty dollars a night as a singer.

ENTRANCE TO ADMINISTRATION BUILDING
WESTERN MICHIGAN COLLEGE
KALAMAZOO, MICHIGAN

KALAMAZOO
SEP 10
9 PM
1959
MICH.

—CURTEICHCOLOR" REPRODUCTION FROM KODACHROME OR EKTACHROME

UNITED STATES POSTAGE 1 CENT

UNITED STATES POSTAGE 1 CENT

POST CARD

Dear Mom and Daddy,

My senior year is off to
a great start. I am now
a student teacher and I am
singing whenever I can. I
am hoping to move to Detroit in May.
I'll be home for Thanksgiving.
Miss you and everyone in Paw Paw.

Love, Loretta

To:
Marjorie and Verle Moore
Rt. 3 Box 259
Paw Paw, Michigan
49079

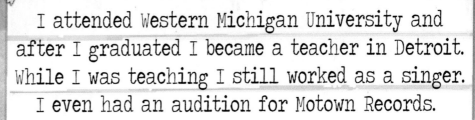

I attended Western Michigan University and after I graduated I became a teacher in Detroit. While I was teaching I still worked as a singer. I even had an audition for Motown Records.

The audition gave me the confidence to move to New York City to continue to occupy my dream.

I want to be a recording artist.

New York City in the early 1960's

POST CARD

NEW YORK, N.Y.
SEP 17
12:30 PM
1961

13

THIS SIDE FOR THE ADDRESS ONLY

Dear Mom and Daddy,
    New York City is so amazing.. I have an audition for a Broadway show tomorrow. I'm living my dream. Miss you!
        Love
        Loretta

DELIVER TO:
PAW PAW, MICHIGAN

BROADWAY

Loretta Long
281-7849
AEA-AFTRA-SAG-AGVA

APOLLO

APOLLO THEATRE
253 West 125th Street
New York City

SEAT 26

ROW LEFT

LOWER MEZZANINE

IT'S SHOWTIME
AT THE
APOLLO THEATRE

THURSDAY, AUGUST 31, 1966

To Do:

1. Get Hair Done
2. Pick Up Dress
3. Rehersal at Apollo
4. Show at 8pm

PBS

August 30, 1968

Dear Loretta,

Welcome aboard!
The first show will air on:
September 12, 1968

Sincerly,
Ellis Haizlip

SOUL! PILOT SCRIPT

Final Draft

Video	Audio
Fade in to Camera 1: CU of Loretta Long	Show tease: Hi! I'm Loretta Long. Stay tuned for the premier episode of Soul! Coming up next right here on WNET Channel 13.

Dr. Edward L. Palmer

6/14/1969

Today I auditioned for a new children's show.

They are showing the tapes to kids.

I hope they like the song I sang.

This would be such a great opportunity.

Loretta

November 11, 1969

Matt Robinson

playing Gordon

To: Staff, Cast, Crew, and all others who work on "Sesame Street."

From: Joan Ganz Cooney

I wanted you to know how aware I am of the contribution that all of you have made in the launching of "Sesame Street."

Each of you has brought essential talents and abilities to the project, but it's your amazing esprit that has made it all work.

Congratulations and many thanks.

'Sesame' Entertainer Reaches For The Stars

Sesame Street's 'Susan' is educator

CHILDREN'S TELEVISION WORKSHOP | NATIONAL EDUCATIONAL TELEVISION

November 30, 1970

Dear Mom and Daddy,

Your prayers are working. The show is a hit! I know it's very hard for you to see it on television back in Paw Paw but the second season has started. Time Magazine is calling the show "TV's Gift to Children".

I am so happy to be a part of it. I hope it lasts forever.
Daddy, how's the antenna working that you built?
Can you see the show now?

I miss everyone back home. Come visit New York City soon.

Love, Loretta

SESAME STREET

TV's Gift to Children

SESAME STREET
8
CANDLES
SUSAN

American Scholars Program

Elementary School in Ghana

POST ☙ CARD

Serie 667;1

Dear Charlie,

This trip has been amazing. When we were kids I never

Greetings from Ghana!

imagined I'd get to travel all over the world I'll be in Detroit at a J.C. Penney's store in two weeks. Gather up Mom, Dad, Cyndi and the kids and come see me !. Love, Loretta

SUSAN SINGS SONGS FROM **SESAME STREET** WITH THE CHILDREN'S CHORUS

October 26, 1970

Dear Mrs. Loretta Long,

We have completed the tabulation of the final balloting by the membership of the National Academy of Recording Arts and Sciences and we are pleased to be able to inform you that you have been voted as a finalist for a Grammy Award in the following category:

Best Record For Children

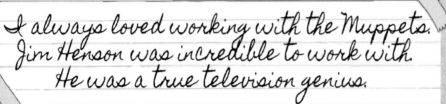

I always loved working with the Muppets. Jim Henson was incredible to work with. He was a true television genius.

Cyndi

Charlie

Marjorie

Doug

Verle

Loretta

Dyana

Dear Leroy,

Today, Loretta was the grand marshal of the Grape Festival Parade. She even rode in front of the same band that she wanted to be in when she was in high school. Look at God!

We are so proud of her. Here are some pictures from her trip back home to Paw Paw.

Love, Your Sister Marjorie

P.S. Dyana wanted the parade to stop when she spotted me!

10 Years...
20 Years...
30 Years...
40 Years...

45 Years
on Sesame Street
and counting...

SUSAN AND GORDON ADOPT MILES

"It gave us a chance to show development of a black child and the love and the parenting skills of a mom and dad. We were able to see them playing with the baby and caring for the baby. It gave a totally different view of Susan and Gordan. It also allowed us to bring in extended family, which is important in African American families."

Dr. Valaria Lovelace,

Head of Research

Sesame Street

Happy Day!
Love, Gordon, Susan, Miles

TEACHING DIVERSITY: THE SESAME STREET METHOD
with Visiting Multicultural Scholar in Residence, Dr. Loretta Long

October 25-29, 2010

Hi Pres,
I look like I belong!

I was the first person in my family to go to college and now I'm speaking at commencement today!

LORETTA (MOORE) LONG
INDUCTED 2000

PAW PAW HIGH SCHOOL HALL OF FAME

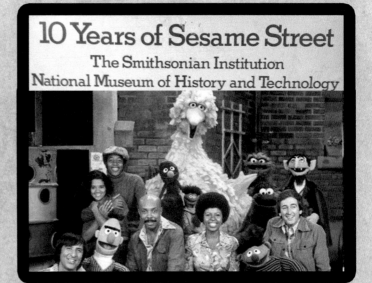

10 Years of Sesame Street
The Smithsonian Institution
National Museum of History and Technology

WESTERN MICHIGAN UNIVERSITY
DISTINGUISHED ALUMNI 1971

Courtney's **BIRTHDAY PARTY**

by Dr. Loretta Long
illustrations by Ron Garnett

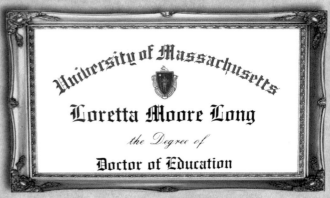

University of Massachusetts
Loretta Moore Long
the Degree of
Doctor of Education

"Life's like a movie,
write your own ending.
Keep believing,
keep pretending."
Jim Henson

Loretta!
I am so happy you were part
of the Carnegie Hall Show.
What a wonderful day!
It meant the world to have
your talent and heart up on
the stage. You are the best.

Love you and Merry Christmas!

Johnny Tartaglia

hollywood bowl

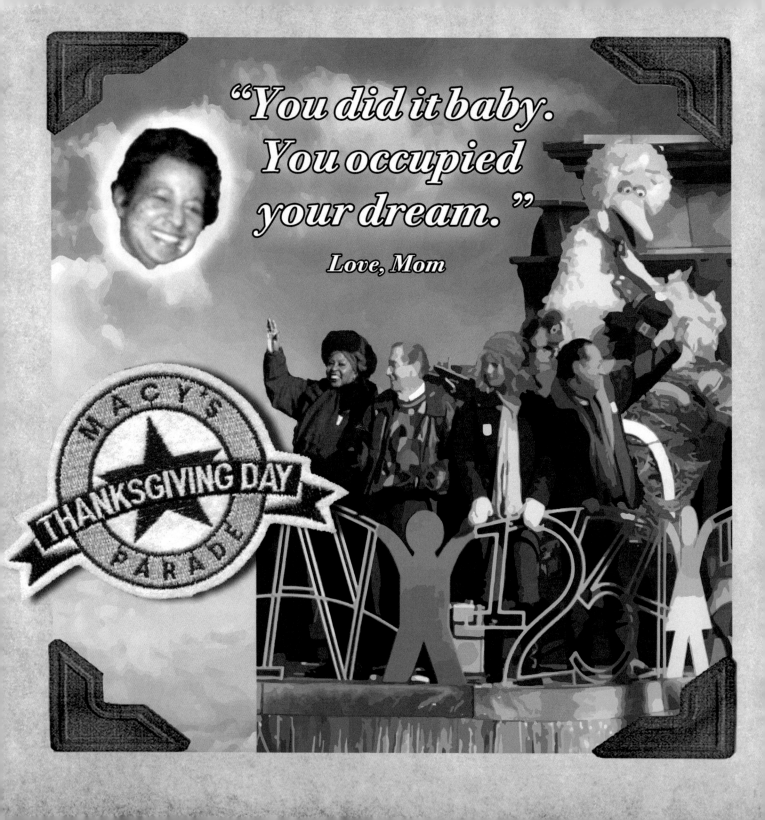

"*You did it baby. You occupied your dream.*"

Love, Mom

MACY'S THANKSGIVING DAY PARADE

Made in the USA
Middletown, DE
04 January 2020